LESSONS FROM AN ELDER FOR THE

NEW GENERATION

A CHANGING WORLD
"FROM AN ELDER'S VIEW"

MARGARET HOSKINS

Professional Publishing House
1425 W. Manchester Ave. Ste. B
Los Angeles, California 90047
323-750-3592
Email: professionalpublishinghouse@yahoo.com
www.Professionalpublishinghouse.com

Cover design: Jay Devance, III
First printing February 2016
978-0-9861557-8-9
10 9 8 7 6 5 4 3 2 1

For inquiries contact: professionalpublishinghouse@yahoo.com

ABOUT THE AUTHOR

$\mathcal{M}$argaret Hoskins was born and raised in Como, Mississippi. She is a seamstress, florist and cake decorator. She is the owner and operator of Hoskins Boutique where she made wedding dresses, flowers, and wedding cakes for all occasions. She is a musician and song writer, writing more than 15 songs and will be making her first CD at the age of 82. She is also writing her first book. She always tells the older adults that it is never too late to realize your dream.

A NOTE FROM THE AUTHOR

I was born in Como, Mississippi. We lived in a small house. It didn't look like much, but it had so much love in it. There are children who live in mansions who wish they could feel the kind of love we felt in this home. This house was truly a home and not just a house and there is a difference.

This little house housed a lot of children. We shared the same bed, and sometimes there were three in a bed. The only problem we had was when one child would pee in the bed some nights. Otherwise, we all got along. We did everything together; we prayed together, worked together, we all went to church together. There was no such thing as "I am not going to church today," in those days.

I mentioned our house to say that we should be grateful for what we have. Thank God. He has blessed us all with nice homes and we have thankful hearts. Over the years, we have shared our homes with many relatives and non-relatives.

DEDICATION

$\mathcal{T}$his book is dedicated to my late father, Simon Hunter, whose imprint is upon each member of the Hunter's family. The word "Hunter" was synonymous to—greatness, smart and daring. That's what our father told us, and we believed whatever our father told us, so here we are today— great, smart, and daring each one of us.

My father was an entrepreneur and that too has passed down through the Hunter's gene. We continue to remind our family members that they are a "Hunter" and Hunter is not just a name, it carries much weight and power such as: You can be whatever you want to be. Never allow others to determine how far you can go in life—it's your determination that counts.

My father's instructions speak from the spirit of the ancestors' realm—we hear you, Daddy. We listen and we obey—it's kinda like you are still here with us—in spirit, you are. Thank you.

ACKNOWLEDGMENTS AND THANKS

First, I want to thank God for allowing me to live these many years and for allowing me the opportunity to pen my story.

I want to thank my sister, Attorney Clara King, for encouraging me to write this book.

I also thank my youngest son, Pastor Ricky Hoskins, and his wife LaLita, for their typing and computer skills used in helping me put this book together.

To my sister Dr. Rosie Milligan AKA Bush Hunter. I thank you for publishing my book and encouraging me to do it—thank you for keeping us all motivated to push and push and push until there is no more push in us.

I want to acknowledge my loving children: my firstborn, Ezzard Charles Hoskins, my daughter-in-law, Linda, my three daughters, Gloria Hoskins, Rosie Chenault, Shirley Lewis and her husband Carl.

I want to acknowledge my sisters and brother, Owen Nelson, Clara King, Dr. Rosie Milligan, Kenyaka Beckley, Lillie Bell Towns, Pastor Johnnie Mae Smith, Robert Earl Hunter, Leroy Hunter and my deceased sisters Willie MiCou, Dotsy Bowden and my deceased brother, Willie Sanders.

TABLE OF CONTENTS

INTRODUCTION

In recent years, I have learned a lot about my ancestors. A lot of the information came from research done by
one of our cousins. As a result of this genealogy search, I
have met and corresponded with many relatives for the first
time and it has greatly enriched my life. In this book, I will
share some of that information and give you a glimpse into
what life was like when I grew up in Mississippi during the
1940s.

My great-grandmother, Mary Reed Pratt, was born in
1850 in Abbeville, South Carolina. Bill Reed, her brother,
was born in 1846 in Abbeville, South Carolina. They were
both born into slavery. Their father, Pleasant Barr, along
with his entire family, was sold to a man named Lemuel

Reed. Since slaves took the last name of their masters, their last names were changed to Reed. After Emancipation, in 1867, they moved with a group of other free people to Panola County in Como, Mississippi. On this journey, they traveled in cover wagons pulled by mules. The master wanted them to stay on with him on the plantation after they were freed from slavery, but they refused. So he gave them a wagon and two mules. Subsequently, they relocated to Como, Mississippi where they worked hard and became very successful.

Grandmother Mary Reed married David Pratt in 1867. David was one of the individuals who came from Abbeville, South Carolina with them. Mary and David Pratt had three children, William Pratt, Sue Pratt, and Louvenia Pratt Hunter. Sue died at a young age. Grandma Mary Pratt died in 1910 at the age of sixty in Como, Mississippi.

Louvenia Pratt Hunter was our paternal grandmother; she was our father, Simon Hunter's mother. She married Grandfather John Allen Hunter in Como, Mississippi in 1885, and they had eight children. Louvenia's brother, William Pratt, moved to Tunica County. His daughter, Lizzie Pratt, came back to Panola County to live with her aunt Louvenia's family. Lizzie was Daddy's first cousin. We all loved her and called her Cousin Lizzie. Grandpa John Allen said that he was a little boy during slavery, therefore, he didn't have much education, but he had wisdom and survival skills. He was a hardworking man. He purchased 160 acres of land, and provided housing for all of his children. When one of his sons or daughters got married, they came to live in the family home. We called it the "Big House".

Grandpa raised cotton, corn, beans, peas, sweet potatoes, popcorn, peanuts, watermelon and sorghum. Many people are not familiar with sorghum. Sorghum is used to make molasses, which is called sorghum molasses and it grows up like corn. Many times we had to help Daddy make more than 300 gallons of molasses. In turn, he divided it with all the neighbors. When it was hog butchering time, Grandpa and Daddy worked together. They always provided meat for the neighbors also. People in the neighborhood would always share their garden produce with others. Grandpa and his children worked on the farm together, they raised hogs, cows, sheep, goats, chickens, turkeys and a variety of horses and mules. We had a wood stove and a wood heater. The women really cooked good food on those old wood stoves; we all loved Grandma's corn bread and sweet potato pie. My mom could make the best chicken and dumpling; we also had a five-acre orchard on the farm that everyone shared.

We had apples, pears, peaches, strawberries, grapes and blackberries. Grandpa would let people come over and help themselves to the blackberries and plums, all the families on the farm sold cream from the milk every week. They would put it in a five-gallon cream can and take it to the depot to be sent to Kankakee, Illinois. In return, they would receive a check by mail. The families all worked together, they sold cows and hogs to the stockyard in Memphis, Tennessee. We sold chickens and eggs, which was an income for us.

Our school in 1940 was a one room school house with one teacher. Our teacher taught every class from the first grade to the eighth grade. My daddy, Simon Hunter, John Henry Simmons and Knowledge Williams were the trustees for our school. They were responsible for providing wood for keeping the school warm. They sawed wood with a manual saw. Grandpa had over 25 acres of wood on his land; he provided wood for the school. Sometimes the teacher had to start the fire in the old wood heater. We did not have gas or electricity in those days. I was 13 years old when we got electricity.

That was the same year we moved from the country school to Carruthers School, and later to Como High School. Some children had to walk two to three miles to the country school. My younger sisters and brothers were blessed to have buses to ride when they became school age. During my first years of school I attended an all-black school. We had prayer every morning and said a bible verse. There were no disobedient children in the school. We all had love and respect for our teacher and for each other.

In 1975, the schools were desegregated in Mississippi, and blacks and whites all attended the same school. In my school days, children sometimes had fist fights, but nobody ever packed a knife or took a gun to school. That was a time when we knew the people in our neighborhoods. We understood, communicated with, and respected each other.

CHAPTER ONE

$\mathcal{U}$nlike today, we now see an increase in racial hatred, violence and brutality, even in the North. And no neighborhood is safe from violence and crime. When knowledge increases trouble increases. This generation has access to a better education than we did, but we didn't have killings in the schools. Our parents didn't have to worry about our fellow students shooting up the classroom.

Consider the following.

- April 20, 1999, in Littleton, Colorado, at Columbine High School, Dyla Klebold and Erick Harris shot and killed 12 students before committing suicide.

- December 14, 2012, in Newtown, Connecticut at Sandy Hook Elementary School, a man open fired and killed 26 people, including 20 children.

- October 2006 in Georgetown, Pennsylvania, Charles Carl Roberts, a 32-year-old milk truck driver, killed 8 little Amish girls in a one room school.

- March 24, 1998 in Jonesboro Arkansas, Mitchell Johnson 13 and Andrew Golden 11, killed four children and one teacher and wounded 10 others at the school. It was after lunch and students had just settled back behind their desk when the fire alarm buzzed.

- February 14, 2008, Stephen Kazmierczak shot and killed 5 people and injured 21 people at Northern Illinois University.

- In April 2014, in Murrysville, Pennsylvania, Alex Hribal, a 16-year-old boy, stabbed and slashed 21 students in the crowded hall of his suburban high school.

- In Mount Morris, Township, Michigan, a 6-year-old boy pulled a gun from his pants and shot a little girl to death in the classroom. The boy fired a bullet from 32 caliber gun inside the elementary school, striking 6-year-old Kayla Rolland in the neck. She died a half hour later. He was the youngest person to use a gun in a school shooting.

Needless to say, guns should be kept away from children; guns should not be kept in a drawer or under the bed. Our children are our most precious gifts from our creator. We owe it to them to take an active role in keeping them safe. We must also take an active interest in their academic development. Reading is one of the most fundamental things that we can teach our children. One of the best ways of doing this is for them to actually see you reading. Have them read the Bible stories while they are young. Some parents start reading to children even while in their wombs during pregnancy. Many begin reading to their children when they are 3 and 4 years of age.

Why It Is Important to Build a Strong Foundation

My daddy always read Bible stories to us when we were young. When we grew older, he taught us how to read and study the bible. He helped us with our school work every day. Daddy always called out our spelling words and then he would have us to write the words down on paper. Daddy was my best math teacher. Some of our children do not bring their books home, but they should. They need to study their lesson over and over if they want to achieve their goals. Black children should not give all their time to the ball games. It is nice for them to participate in the school games, but only after they finish their daily school work and are advancing in academics. Everybody is not going to be a star; however, everyone can be good at something in life. In the past, some people didn't have much education, but they invented things that made a positive impact and enriched the lives of many people.

If everyone were a doctor, what would we do for a mortician? If everyone were a beautician, what would we do for a carpenter? If everyone were to sing in the choir, what would we do for a preacher who brings the Gospel? The point is we all have God given talents, but some have buried theirs.

For this reason, I tell young people as they go off to college, they must remember two things; don't forget your creator and don't forget the bridge that brought you across.

In the beginning there was the family where home is a child's first school. Children need to learn mother wit and wisdom before college. With a basic foundation, a willingness to work hard, and common sense, people can accomplish great things.

CHAPTER TWO

Although Black people did not have much education, they were creative and used their God-given ability to accomplish and invent many things.

Look at some of these inventors:

- In 1871, a black man M.R. Demortie organized a Richmond Virginia Company, which establish a sassafras oil factory.

- In 1985, Seaway National Bank of Chicago was the largest Black owned bank with assets of 103 million.

- In 1994, William A. Hinton was the first black to become a professor at Harvard medical School.

- In 1929, Arthur Herdon was the only black candy manufactory in America.

- In 1890, Reverend W.R. Pettiford organized the Alabama Penny Savior Band of Birmingham Alabama.

- In 1876, a black owned and operated a Buggy Manufacturing company.

- In 1893, Southern Aid Society was the oldest industrial insurance company operated by blacks.

- In 1970, one thousand and fifty-one black women doctors were counted in the U.S.

- In 1827, the Freedom Journal published the first black newspaper.

- In 1910, Madame C. J. Walker became the first black female millionaire. 1773 James Durham was the first regularly recognized black physician in the United States.

- In 1893, Daniel Hale Williams performed the world's first successful heart operation. Moreover, the open heart surgery was performed at a hospital founded by Williams.

- In 1940, Charles Drew, M. D., was the first person to set up a blood bank. He discovered methods of processing and storing blood plasma for blood transfusion.

- In 1916, Frederick Douglass Patterson was the first black to manufacture cars.

- In 1940, Frederick McKinley was the man to invent a practical refrigeration system for trucks and railroad cars.

- On September 12, 1992, Chicago, Illinois, Mae C. Jemison became the first Black women to travel into outer space.

- In 1898, Lydia Neuman, a Black woman, invented the first hair brush with synthetic bristles.

- Joseph N. Jackson invented the television remote control.

- Otis Boykin invented a wide range of electronic devices, including a resistor used in many computers, radios and televisions. His most famous invention was a control unit for the pacemaker. Granville T. Woods invented Synchronous Multiplex Railway Telegraph.

These are only some of the documented inventions that Blacks created. There are many more inventions that weren't patented, and truth be known, were stolen by white society.

CHAPTER THREE

Black History

*L*et's go back to the beginning of the diaspora's journey in America. The history of Black America began when a ship carrying 20 blacks landed in Jamestown, Virginia. The first African Americans arrive in the United States in 1619. Blacks have come a long way since that fateful day of 1619.

Fast forward. In 2008, we elected our first black president in the United States, the honorable President Barack Obama. His lovely wife is named Michelle and they have two daughters, Malia and Sasha. Barack attended Columbia University in 1983 with a major in Political Science, and later attended Harvard Law School. He was the first African American elected as president of the Harvard Law Review in 1990. That position is considered the highest student position at Harvard Law School. In 1995, Mr. Obama published his first book, *Dreams From my Father*, a story of race and inheritance, and in 2006, he published The *Audacity of Hope*. President Obama wanted to help sick people that could not afford insurance because he had a heart and cared about his country and people. That is why he made it possible for people to have health insurance.

In 1935, when many people in America were homeless and unemployed, President Franklin Delano Roosevelt signed the Social Security Act and laid the foundation of a system that has been a lifeline to the elderly. In 1961, President John F. Kennedy started the economy moving again. People were able to get jobs. Under his presidency, he made it possible for adults to go back to school. I, myself, went back to school at the age of 44 and graduated with an applied science associates degree from Danville Area Community College. I graduated along with my oldest daughter.

Afterwards, my daughter and I worked in the school as Teacher's Aids. Some went back to school at 50 to 60 years of age, some students dropped out of school, but they were able to go back and get their G.E.D. and go on to college. Nobody should be idle; opportunity does not knock on your door every day. Schools used to teach homemaking that was good for the students. They learned practical skills how to sew and cook.

Unfortunately, today, most young parents do not know how to cook. They love pizza, hamburgers and fries. They seldom eat a nutritious meal. Often the family cannot all eat together because the teenagers have a job or maybe Daddy is at work. It's no wonder families are falling apart.

CHAPTER FOUR

Suggestions for Building Stronger Families

We need to go back to the "old school" methods of rearing children. For example, we must teach our children good table manners, and teach them to say grace. Children should be encouraged to eat their meals first, and then watch TV. Too often, modern children are eating, watching TV, and wrestling with siblings, at the same time. The dinner table should be a time of coming together as a family and sharing your day.

When we were children, we ate what our parents gave us. Today, children all want something different at each meal. The mother scrambles to prepare something different for each child at their request. If parents did not allow children to give orders as if they at a restaurant, they may learn to eat a little of everything on the table. They may find that they like things they have never tried before.

Parents should decide what type of programs children should watch on television and they should monitor and limit the amount of time spent in watching T.V. Children should have a set time to watch television. It is good for some small children to watch cartoons, but take some time to talk to them, and read stories to them.

In the Bible, Deuteronomy says: "Thou shalt teach them when thou sittest in thine house and when thou walkest by the way and when thou liest down, and when thou riseth up."

See, children need adult guidance in order to reach their full and best potential. Child rearing is not something children can do for themselves. You can't know what you haven't been taught. The Bible gives the best instruction for rearing children. Isaiah 54:13 says, "All thy children shall be taught of the Lord, and great shall be the peace of thy children."

Proverbs 22:26 says, "Foolishness is bound in the heart

of a child, but the rod of correction shall drive it far from them."

Proverbs 29:15 says, "A child left to himself bringeth his mother to shame."

Children with no training or teaching in the home will become perverse. Children can grow up thinking of themselves as inferior to other children and will behave accordingly. As a result, their self-evaluation becomes a self-reinforcing and a self-fulfilling prophecy.

As the old proverbial saying goes, "As the twig is bent, so is the tree inclined."

CHAPTER FIVE

The State of Children Who Were Raised by Addicted Parents

*S*ome children today have bad behavior because their mom and dad were on drugs. Far too often, their grandpa and grandma were also on drugs. It is not the children's fault; they cannot be held accountable for what the parents did to them. When children are taken out of a home because their parents abuse drugs, the parents should at least be court-ordered to go to the home and help care for their children. The mother should do the girls' hair, and both parents should be required to spend supervised visits with the children at least twice a week. It would make the child feel better, even if they know the visit is forced.

Children love their parents and want to spend time with them and feel like their parents care about them. All foster children are not drug babies. Some parents do not take proper care of their children, which is why they are taken out of the home. My daughter, Gloria, has two children of her own; over the years, she adopted 4 other children and took care of 20 more foster children in her home while working at the Danville Correction Center. She has a great love for children. The state does not pay enough money to take care of these children, because I have kept 4 foster children myself. I brought clothes for them so they could look nice. I do not think anyone is keeping the foster children for the money. Most people are doing it out of the goodness of their heart. Some of these children were taken from their parents because their mother had marijuana in her system. Does anyone check to see if the foster parents have marijuana in their system?

A child should not be taken from the home just because a parent smokes marijuana, especially if the parents are taking care of their children and no child is abused in the home. There are so many single mothers these days. We see babies having babies while grandmothers and grandfathers are often left to care of them. It does take a village to raise a child.

Proverbs 30:11 says, "There is a generation that curse their father, and do not bless their mother." The disrespect we see in children and teens for their parents and other elders today is so unlike what it was like in former years. When we were children and acted up, all the adult had to say was "I am going to tell your daddy," and we got our act together.

We need more workshops for our young parents. If we reach the parents, we can reach the children. Parents should be consistent with their children and teach them to respect authority, beginning at home. If children don't respect their parents, they won't respect their teachers and their employers or the police. Without the proper respect, they are headed for trouble.

Women should teach their girls about sex. If there is no man in the home, they should teach their boys also. Teach young people to prepare themselves to make a living before they start having sex. Girls and boys should get their education first. The next step should be getting a job. After this they are ready to get married and have children. Young men need to know a man's responsibility; 1 Timothy 5:8. "But if anyone does not provide for his own, and especially for those of his household, he has denied the faith and is worse than an unbeliever."

More males drop out of school than females. If a young woman drops out of school, she will find a job and work, but, most young men will hang out on the street corner, sell drugs and commit crimes. Most of them have guns, and, consequently, a great number of African American men are incarcerated in the criminal justice system.

Therefore, many children are raised without a father in their life. Nonetheless, we have a lot of African American men who graduate from college every year, have good jobs or have their own business. You can tell the difference between an intelligent, self-respecting man and a lazy, ignorant man. You can tell by the way they dress, and by the way they talk. I am sick of people talking about black-on-black crimes. I am not minimizing the fact that Blacks are being killed on the street and in drive-by shootings, but what about white-on-white crime? White men are shooting up the schools, the shopping malls and also theatres. They are killing 20 to 40 people at a time.

One has to understand that this is a spiritual war. Satan is on a rampage. America has its own war within America. Too many unstable people have access to guns. Hatred, racism and violence are on the increase and the love of many have waxed cold.

When Dr. King was teaching and preaching non-violence, people did not take it seriously. When we were children, my daddy and all the men had shot guns in a rack on the wall. They would all get together and go hunting. Back then, children did not think of touching a gun. However, if men left their guns out in the open like that today, everybody in the neighborhoods would be shot.

CHAPTER SIX

Homebased Businesses that
Never Go Out of Style

In 1940, many people in the country did not have telephones in their homes. If someone got sick, they had to walk for miles or ride a horse to use a phone to call the doctor. In our neighborhood, John Turner was a kind white man who would let people come in his home, any time of night, to use his phone to call the doctor. When older people were sick, the doctor would make home visits.

As of today, technology has make it possible for people to have all kinds of phones. We have Galaxy, I-Phones, Kindles, Ipads, working and talking phones, Obama phones.

Everybody in the house has his own phone. We have snapchat, Facetime, Face Book and Twitter. Technology is good, but it has divided the family. Parents do not have time to communicate with each other, nor their children. When they are in a car, they are talking on a phone or texting.

People use to travel in a wagon. My friend said when she was a child, her daddy took her to the hospital in a wagon. My uncle Frank and his wife always rode in their buggy. In 1950, people had one car per home. Today parents have their cars and all the children have their own cars.

Some have Mercedes, Cadillacs, Rolls Royce, BMW's and Lexus, but people are still unhappy and do not have any joy. They have tried to use material things to fill an emptiness in their spirit.

Let us look at the work force. I came to Danville, Ohio in 1960. I was 26 years old. My first job was at Hotel Worford. I made 50 cents an hour. My sister and I lived together. We lived in a one room house with a kitchen. We walked to work every day, we did not have food stamps or a medical card. It was a good thing that we did not get sick. I am a witness that God will make a way out of no way. We moved from a one- bedroom house to a three bedroom. By that time my wages were $3.00 an hour. After that, we both were able to move into our own home. Sometimes you have to crawl before you can walk. After I lost my job in 1980, I went to Danville Community College and took up floral arrangements.

The first person I made wedding flowers for was my niece. My business started then. I got calls from all over town. People wanted me to do their weddings, but also, they wanted flowers for all occasions. My sister, Dr. Rosie Milligan, came from Los Angeles, CA. and helped us to organize a Business Opportunity Group. I made flowers for Danville, Champaign, also mailed flowers out of town. I also made flower dresses, head pieces, bride's maid dresses and clothes for all occasions. My sister, Owen Nelson, also sews and make cakes for weddings and all occasions. She decorated the most beautiful wedding cakes. My sister, Willie Micou, made quilts and ordered shoes for people. This gift runs in the family. My relatives, Macie Lillard and Gloria Hoskins, both catered food for weddings and all occasions. Betty Ann Gouard made wedding dresses and bride maid dresses and sewed for all occasions.

Our Business Opportunity Group served the community for 3 decades. Two of our members are deceased and we are all senior citizens now. Even so, we are trying to start up a new business opportunity group to serve the community.

People can start a small business in their home. Throughout our history, beautician work is the biggest work for African American women. I see women cut their hair off. The next month, they buy some long hair and have it put on their head. The next month, they take it off and have some braids put on. The cost for hair braiding is $200.00.

There is a great need for seamstresses all the time. One can make good money just altering clothes and hemming pants, dresses and skirts. Teenagers can start a small business. Many have good typing skill and know how to operate the computer. People need typing all the time. Young boys can cut grass for the family.

Another area people can contribute their services is through volunteer work. Parents should encourage their children to serve as volunteers. The question, "Why do you volunteer?" is often asked of volunteers, and there is no simple answer. Each volunteer has his or her own unique reason for being involved. There are activities any family can do that not only help others, but also build stronger, healthier, more joyful relationships between parents and children.

These are some of the reason people volunteer to serve:

- An attitude of openness

- A willingness to seek out new experiences and not wait for them to come to you

- A readiness to help

- An attitude of acceptance of different people and situations.

- A belief that learning is meant to be life long and that we can in fact learn from others.

CONCLUSION

These are the descendants of John Allen Hunter and Louvenia Hunter: James Frank Hunter, Mary Hunter Watkins, Robert Hunter, Nelson Hunter, Lucile Hunter Howard, Allen Bell Hunter Webb and Simon Owen Hunter.

"And thy seed shall be as the dust of the earth, and thou shalt spread abroad to the west, and to the east, and to the north, and to the south, and in thee, and in thy seed shall all the families of the earth be blessed."
—Genesis 28:14.

The Hunter family is a loving family. They always worked together on the farm and all their children went to the same church. Children would walk miles to church and Sunday School. My daddy, Simon Hunter, was a Sunday School teacher, a deacon and the secretary of the Hunter Chapel Baptist Church for many years. Mr. Robert Gibson was the Sunday School Superintendent for 38 years.

When I was 17 years old, I had an experience I will never forget. It was the day I was sponsoring my first program at the church. I was so happy, and my mom was planning on going to the program. My mom was combing my little sister Kenyaka's hair. She told me and my sister, Willie, that she did not feel good. As she started to the bed to lay down, she fell. We tried to pick her up. My brother, Robert Earl, ran to Mr. Otis Turner's house and asked him to help us get mom up from the floor. But there was nothing anyone could do. She had died of a heart attack.

That was the saddest day I ever had in my life. Daddy had gone to the store to buy groceries. Mom had a 4 month-old baby named Moses; sadly, he lived only 3 months after her death. My older sister, Willie, and I had to take on the mom role in helping raise the younger children. My oldest sister, Owen, was married, but she was there for us. We had a Christian Daddy. He sat us all down and talked to us, telling us to be a strong, close family and God was going to see us through.

After 4 years, Daddy married Mrs. Zulena Jennings. She had a son named Willie B. and daughter named Nelie Bell. She was a good stepmother and we were a happy family again. I am a witness that the Lord will make a way, because I couldn't see any way that we could have lived without a mom.

When we were children, our families all lived in the same town. Some of them relocated to Memphis, but that was not too far away. In 1943, some of the young men went to the Army during World War II, and some moved to the city, seeking better employment opportunities and a better quality of life.

In 1955, my brother, Robert Earl, after leaving the Army, came home for a while, then he moved to Los Angeles California. In 1957, my youngest brother, Leroy, moved to Los Angeles. After my sister, Clara, graduated from Como High School, she attended college in Mississippi for one year. During the summer, she went to Los Angles to visit my brother, Leroy, and decided to stay and attend college in Los Angeles. My sister, Rosie, moved from Como to Danville, Illinois before she finished high school. After a year, she moved to California, where she finished her last year of high school. My youngest sister, Kenyaka, graduated from Como High School and spent a year in Danville before moving to Los Angeles. All five of them settled in L.A. My daddy said that he was sorry that they were all so far from home.

In the old days, when parents were no longer able to take care of themselves, their children would move in and care for them. Many, who had left the state looking for better opportunities, had to move back home. Older people who have lived in a town all of their lives find it hard to adjust to another place. When they leave their home to live with their children, they are constantly asking their children to take them back home. For most of them, going back home is always on their mind.

Let's look at the changing times. In the 1915's, there was no foster parents. Families took care of their own children. Some of them had twelve and thirteen children. Kids would visit their grandparents, but parents raised their own children. We loved to visit our grandparents, but when night came, we were at home.

Our ancestors worked hard so that we could have a brighter day. Parents sent their children to college, there were no government loans, grants, or scholarships available. They also had to pay room and board. Many young people who go to college today spend more time partying, doing drugs and drinking than studying. As a result, their education falls by the wayside. It really breaks a parent's heart when they have sacrificed and sent their children to college, yet they never obtain a degree. Many just drop out and come back home, leaving the parents with disappointment and a tuition bill to pay.

It's time for adults to stop talking about what their daddy did or didn't do for them. You are grown now. Get up and do something yourself. What are you doing for your own children? Men have destroyed their mind, wrecked their lives and practiced unspeakable cruelties against one another based on hurts of the past. When a person clings to the pain and frustration of their childhood and refuse to see or move beyond it, they forget that they are no longer a child.

II Corinthians 17 states, "Therefore, if any man be in Christ he is a new creature, old things are passed away, all things become new." I Corinthians 3:11 states, "When I was a child, I spake as a child, I understood as a child, I thought as a child, but when I became a man, I put away childish things."

The past is behind you; you can't change it. The future is before you. What will you do with it? If you make a decision to lay your hurts aside, your future will be brighter and your life more fulfilling.

Dr. King tried very hard to teach the world about love and nonviolence. We can see today that many people in America are wicked, and are living in perilous times. When Dylan Storm Roof, a 21-year-old white supremacist, showed up at a Bible study at Emanuel African Methodist Episcopal Church in Charleston, South Carolina, the congregation welcomed him. At the end of the service, he pulled out his pistol and killed 9 people. He claimed that what he read on the Internet about black people are taking over the world, led him to believe that he had to do something about it. The blood of those innocent people are on the hands of the white supremacy organizations that poisoned his mind.

We hear people talking about taking our country back. The first chapter of Genesis says: "In the beginning, God created the heavens and the earth." Psalms 24 says, "The earth is the Lord's and the fullness thereof; the world and they that dwell therein." Job 1:21 says: "Naked came I into this world, and naked will I depart."

No matter how much you can accumulate by working, saving, investing, or stealing from others, when you leave here, you will not take any of it with you. How much money you have may give you access to a better life. It may also increase the length of your life due to all the advantages it brings, but Hebrews 9:27 says: "It is appointed unto man once to die, but after this the judgment."

Men are trying to change God's laws. The bible says let every man have his own wife and every woman have her own husband, but the state laws allow man to "have it his way." We see many states issuing marriage license to same sex couples. While same sex couples are fighting for the right to marry, men and women are living together without any intent of getting married. No one wants to obey God's laws. Now the states are giving foster children to lesbian and homosexuals to raise, and some of them can adopt children.

It is a shame and a disgrace for children to be raised in a home with same sex couples. God loves everybody, but God hates sin. No one should hate gays or lesbians; we all have sinned, 1 John 1-18 says, "If we say we have no sin, we deceive ourselves, and the truth is not in us. If we confess our sins, He is faithful and just to forgive us our sins, and cleanse us from all unrighteousness. If we say that we have not sinned, we make him a liar, and His word is not in us." Proverbs 6:10 says, "These are the 3 of the six things doth the Lord hate: a proud look, a lying tongue, a hand that shed innocent blood." People can be delivered from their sins, but they must be willing or have a desire to change. God created us as free moral agents with the ability to make our own decisions. Focus your eyes on God, rather than on your problems. 1 John 4:11 says, "Whosoever hateth his brother is a murderer."

We can see today that people in the church, including preachers, hate people because of their race. If anybody hate me, they hated God first.

Matthew 5:44 says, "Love your enemies, bless them that curse you, do good to them that hate you, and pray for them which despitefully use you and persecute you." Who will be able to pass the test-nobody but a born again Christian? If we all cannot live together on this earth down here and love one another, we all will perish as fools.

Dr. King once said, "I cannot make myself believe that God wants me to hate. We have a power that cannot be found in bullets and guns. We, as a black race, should not worry so much about reparation. There is nothing that can compensate for the wrong and evil of slavery and more than two hundred years of injustice. We have learned that the virtue of forgiveness outweighs the burden of vengeance, because vengeance belongs to God. So let us look at it as a dark era of our history and let us look forward to a sun lighted path of sisterhood and brotherhood. The scripture teaches us that God made man in his own image. I do not believe that there is any such thing as irreconcilable differences.

"God does not show favoritism based on the color of your skin or status in life, if you think He does, read the obituaries or visit the cemeteries. We must never forget that the creator is in charge of everything and is the author of life and death for everybody. There is a court that is higher than the Supreme Court. One day we will all stand before the righteous judge, and every man will be judged according to his works. If we let love rang, we will be able to overcome racial and religious bigotry and the bright beautiful sunlight and twinkling starlight of love will shine over our great nation and we will be able to really come together as one nation, under God. We are looking forward to that day when the Heavenly Father will say to those who put their trust in Him, well done, my good and faithful servant."

www.ingramcontent.com/pod-product-compliance
Lightning Source LLC
Chambersburg PA
CBHW021914040426

42447CB00007B/853